Remembering
Orlando

Joy Wallace Dickinson

TURNER
PUBLISHING COMPANY

A view of Orange Avenue looking north from Church Street shows the First National Bank building at left and the side of Ivey's of Orlando on the right. Based in Charlotte, North Carolina, this department-store chain was founded by J. B. Ivey, a devout Methodist who required that the curtains on his store windows be drawn on Sundays, so that pedestrians would not be tempted by worldly matters on the Lord's day.

Remembering
Orlando

Turner Publishing Company
4507 Charlotte Avenue • Suite 100
Nashville, Tennessee 37209
(615) 255-2665

Remembering Orlando

www.turnerpublishing.com

Library of Congress Control Number: 2010923503

ISBN: 978-1-59652-633-4

Printed in the United States of America

ISBN: 978-1-68336-868-7 (pbk)

10 11 12 13 14 15 16—0 9 8 7 6 5 4 3 2 1

CONTENTS

A woman shows off the popularity of equestrian sports in the Orlando area in a Department of Commerce image from 1946. During the mid twentieth century, the Canadian-born horseman Ben White made Orlando the world's foremost training center for harness racing, at the now-gone track named for him, Ben White Raceway.

ACKNOWLEDGMENTS

This volume, *Remembering Orlando,* is the result of the cooperation and efforts of many individuals and organizations.

Thanks, as always, to the work of fellow historians Mark Andrews, Ben Brotemarkle, Gary Mormino, Tana Porter, Steve Rajtar, and Jim Robison for information and inspiration, and to the staff of the Orange County Regional History Center and the "history warriors" of Orlando Remembered, happy guardians of a proud heritage. I am grateful to Martha Link Yesowitch for her keen editorial assistance and to Glenn Link for support and wise counsel.

Few venerable sayings are as true as the one about a picture and a thousand words. Historians and residents of Florida owe a great debt to the creators and staff of the Florida Photographic Collection at the State Archives in Tallahassee, the source of the fascinating images in the pages that follow and one of the state's great treasures (see www.floridamemory.com).

The state's photo archive has benefited from components such as the MOSAIC Photo Collection, with more than 1,000 images of Jewish life in Florida that have been placed in the Florida Photographic Collection by the Jewish Museum of Florida in Miami. Such sharing of images and information enriches the heritage of a great and varied state.

—*Joy Wallace Dickinson*

With the exception of touching up imperfections that have accrued with the passage of time and cropping where necessary, no changes have been made. The focus and clarity of many images are limited to the technology and the ability of the photographer at the time they were recorded.

The goal in publishing this work is to provide broader access to a set of extraordinary photographs. The aim is to inspire, provide perspective, and evoke insight that might assist officials and citizens, who together are responsible for determining Orlando's future. In addition, the book seeks to preserve the past with respect and reverence. We encourage readers to reflect as they explore Orlando, stroll along its streets, or wander its neighborhoods. It is the publisher's hope that in making use of this work, longtime residents will learn something new and that new residents will gain a perspective on where Orlando has been, so that each can contribute to its future.

—*Todd Bottorff, Publisher*

PREFACE

Those of us who have had the opportunity to live for a spell in the older neighborhoods of Orlando, Florida, know this familiar scenario: Friends and family members come to visit, and along with the obligatory and much-anticipated excursions to the area's famous theme parks, the host or hostess may slip in a ride around town.

Passing over brick-paved streets and beneath old oaks draped with Spanish moss, the Orlando resident will show off many lakeside scenes and plenty of houses with roots early in the twentieth century—houses that would be at home in any pretty town in America. There are Craftsman-style bungalows, Spanish Revival mansions, and even a few Victorian gems—homes that have harbored a city's hopes and dreams for generations. And it's a good bet that at some point the out-of-towners will invariably exclaim, "My goodness, I had no idea Orlando looked like this!"

They have no idea because, although it often seems that everyone in the world has visited Orlando, a relatively small percentage of these good folks see the actual city. Perhaps the biggest challenge facing those of us who enjoy rummaging through the city's history is making the case that Orlando does in fact have a history B.D., or "Before Disney," as local history buffs like to call it.

Walt was following a historic trend, of course, when he picked the Orlando area to be the home of Walt Disney World, the second and much larger attraction that in 1971 followed his Disneyland in California. Indeed, the earliest non-Indian settlers in Central Florida in the two decades before the Civil War were drawn by exactly what attracted Disney when he looked down at Central Florida from an airplane in November 1963 and saw the intersection of two major highways and, more important, empty land. Lots of land, under sunny skies above.

Wild Florida has always had as much in common with the Wild West as with the Old South, and in the mid and late nineteenth century, the palmetto prairies at its center beckoned to cattlemen from Georgia and elsewhere. South they rolled on wagons and on steamboats heading up the great St. Johns River, in search of a fresh start in the frontier land of the flowers. Very soon, folks from the north who heard of the joys of a Florida winter also traveled south in search of better health. Although its role as a tourist mecca has come in the years since Disney's opening, the Orlando area has long had its share of sojourners from colder climes.

Some, such as Western photographer Stanley J. Morrow, whose work you'll see in the pages that follow, left a legacy in images that offers proof indeed that Orlando existed and prospered long before there was a Walt Elias Disney, God bless him.

And by the way, think about this as you start your photographic journey through Orlando's past. Walt, who was born in 1901, narrowly missed being a Floridian himself. His parents were married not far from Orlando in Lake County, Florida, in 1888.

Especially during the Florida land boom of the 1920s, gates indicating new subdivisions sprang up all around Orlando and Central Florida, bearing lavish names designed to lure Northern investors. This 1915 sign for Bellevue "Heights" is especially amusing when one considers that the Orlando area's elevation is about 110 feet above sea level. With a few exceptions, a slight rise in the road constitutes a "height" in Orlando.

Rise of the Phenomenal City

(1880s–1908)

"Florida Crackers," reads a handwritten description of two men in an oxcart in early Orlando on the reverse of this image. Unlike usage sometimes considered an epithet, "Cracker" in Central Florida connotes hardy pioneer roots, fierce independence, and often a heritage of raising cattle in the palmetto prairie.

The Daily Record (left), on Pine Street looking east in the 1880s, carried the slogan "A phenomenal daily published in a phenomenal city." At one point Charles Lord owned the grocery across from the Record (note the Y.M.C.A. sign next to it). About 1910, Lord imported swans from his native England and placed them in Lake Lucerne as a gift to the city. They would become an Orlando trademark.

"Big Tom" Shine's Magnolia Hotel, built in 1881 on the west side of Orange Avenue between Central and Pine streets, became a leading social center in Orlando during the 1880s. A cousin of Captain Thomas J. Shine, "Big Tom" served three terms in the Florida legislature. In later years the second-floor veranda of his hotel served as a bandstand for concerts by the Orlando Cornet Band.

Horse-drawn wagons travel along Court Street in photographer Stanley J. Morrow's view looking south from the top of the block-wide brick Armory Building between Pine and Church streets. The steeple of the Methodist Church at Main and Jackson streets is in the background at left; the Opera House is the roof in front of the church.

Two men perch on a rooftop in photographer Stanley J. Morrow's panoramic view of Orlando rooftops about 1886 looking northwest from the Armory building. In the 1870s, Morrow had honed his skills in the West, where he photographed gold-rush towns, soldiers, and American Indians.

Stanley J. Morrow's panoramic shot looking southwest from the roof of Orlando's Armory building in the mid-1880s shows a livery stable and plenty of room for mules and horses near the city center. The commercial center of early Orlando, the Armory housed a huge farmers' market on the ground floor, run by the city, which ruled that no one could sell fresh produce in town except at the Armory.

A sailboat skims along a banana-tree-lined Lake Concord in the mid-1880s. Decades later, busy Interstate 4 crosses over the lake near the commercial center of Orlando.

Stanley J. Morrow's iconic image of a "Cracker" with reptile, in front of Sinclair's Real Estate Agency at Orange Avenue and Pine Street about 1885, has inspired a life-size statue outside the Orange County Regional History Center in downtown Orlando, only a few blocks from the spot where the picture was taken.

This panorama by Stanley Morrow, facing northeast from the Armory building, captures Orlando's 1880s transformation from woods to land-boom frontier town. During the 1880s, investors in Florida land advertised heavily in England and attracted settlers with the prospect of becoming gentlemen citrus growers. The ornate Victorian building that housed the English social club (not shown in this view) remains a landmark in downtown Orlando.

Stanley Morrow's mid-1880s vista looking southeast from Orlando's Armory building shows brick chimneys on the Armory, the Orlando Pipe Works (center), and Lake Lucerne, an early center of prominent homes, in the distance. After the Armory was torn down about 1930, Central Florida architect James Gamble Rogers II used bricks from the building in one of his masterworks, the home later called Casa Feliz in Winter Park.

Now bisected by a causeway bearing a main thoroughfare into Orlando's downtown, Lake Lucerne in the booming 1880s was the developing site of large homes and the Lucerne Hotel (center). To the right of the hotel, the Norment-Parry House, built in 1883, is said to be Orlando's oldest home and is part of a bed-and-breakfast inn, the Courtyard at Lake Lucerne.

Built in 1881, the Lucerne Hotel burned in 1886, probably not long after photographer Stanley J. Morrow recorded this image. Orlando was home to several hotels in the late 1800s that welcomed winter visitors and new residents to the city that boosters bragged was "built on the peel of an orange."

Stanley J. Morrow called this photo "two ponds." This may be lakes Cherokee and Davis, two neighboring lakes that have merged in times of heavy rains and flooding. Since its earliest settlement, Orlando's many lakes have offered a key attraction to visitors and new residents.

Crowds of people, many carrying umbrellas or parasols, flock to Orlando's fairgrounds beside Lake Eola for the first agricultural exposition in 1886. The fair was on the north side of the lake, not far from the side of the band shell that provides a venue for performances and concerts.

The Orlando area's first agricultural fair took place in 1886 on the shores of Lake Eola, around a wooden structure (at left) that the city built in 1885 on the lake's west side, near the present-day site of the Rosalind Club. The annual Central Florida Exposition, which continues today, traces its roots to the 1886 event.

Orlando celebrates Independence Day with a flag-bedecked parade moving east on West Church Street about 1886. The large sign at bottom right bears the name of businessman G. W. Papot, who a few years later opened an orange-box factory powered by a steam engine with a boiler.

A man and child stand at the gate of a neatly fenced yard around an Orlando residence in the mid-1880s, in another of photographer Stanley J. Morrow's scenes of the city.

A wagon heads south on Orlando's Orange Avenue in the mid-1880s. Eventually Orange became downtown's main commercial street, but in the city's early years, before a conflagration swept through much of downtown in 1884, Pine Street served as the main business corridor.

The single, horse-drawn car of the Orlando Street Railway Company pulls away from the South Florida Railroad Company Station on West Church Street about 1886, the year the railway station was built. Hardware merchant Joseph Bumby's two-story brick building (center) also dates from 1886 and remains one of the oldest structures in Orlando. In July 1886, Orlando's city council stipulated that the streetcar must not go more than six miles an hour.

Photographer Stanley Morrow's view looking north on Orange Avenue at Church Street in the late 1880s shows Cassius A. Boone's hardware store at right and skins hanging outside Nicholson's "Menagerie" at left. The woman crossing the street is thought to be Mrs. Metcalf, the beautiful wife of a local saloon-keeper.

Oranges cover the ground after the freeze of 1886, the first significant crop-damaging assault by cold on modern Central Florida citrus growers. Ice at Pine and Main streets downtown on Saturday, December 27, did not disappear until the following Wednesday. The harm done to the budding citrus industry in 1886 was mild compared with the great freeze that was to come in 1894-95.

Photographer H. A. Abercromby recorded this flooded section of Orlando sometime in the 1880s or 1890s, according to Florida State Archives records. During heavy rains, the area near Greenwood Cemetery and the black community of Jonestown, east of downtown Orlando, was especially prone to flooding.

State delegates to the World's Fair Convention assemble at Orlando's Opera House on October 7, 1891. The fourth person from the right on the front row is thought to be Florida governor Francis P. Fleming; fifth from the right is his wife, Florida Lydia Pearson, the daughter of state supreme court justice Bird M. Pearson. Fleming, a Confederate veteran from the Jacksonville area, was Florida's fifteenth governor, from 1889 to 1893.

H. A. Abercromby probably photographed this church group in Orlando or neighboring Winter Park in the 1890s. The newspaper displayed by the man on the front row (second from right) is the *Winter Park Advocate*, published by and for members of the black community.

A bird's-eye view of a lakeside orange grove in 1904 shows an idyllic Florida landscape just as English colonists who tried their hand at orange growing in the Orlando area might have imagined it. The great freeze of 1894-95 and its devastation of area citrus groves sent many of them back to the mother country. By the time this photograph was made a decade later, the citrus industry was making a comeback in Orange County.

Shade trees and homes line Orlando's Magnolia Avenue about 1900. Originally the street was named Magnolia only from Livingston Avenue north. In the 1960s, the old Main Street was renamed Magnolia, extending it south from Livingston to Lake Lucerne. It is now a busy thoroughfare leading from downtown to a main entrance to Interstate 4.

Rising out of a rustic landscape, the 1892 courthouse caused some residents to wonder "what in the world would little Orlando and Orange County do with such a tremendous building?" In time, it became a beloved landmark; Orlando children learned to count by hearing its bell toll the hour. It was torn down in the 1950s, a time of infatuation with the modern in Florida; in later years, when historic buildings came to be more appreciated, it might have been preserved.

Palmettos and trees hung with Spanish moss line Orlando's South Orange Avenue in 1902. Named early in the city's history because it ended in an orange grove on the north end, Orange Avenue would become the city's main downtown thoroughfare, called "the Drag" by students at Orlando High School in the 1940s and early 1950s.

Large homes and a tree-lined walkway surround Lake Lucerne in 1904. Now bisected by a causeway, the lake was the focus of Orlando's central park before Lake Eola took that role later in the twentieth century. Lake Lucerne was originally named Lake Lucindy after Mrs. Barnard Hughey, whose family homesteaded on the western shore in the late 1850s. Early city leader Cassius Boone rechristened it after the famous Lake Lucerne in Switzerland.

This grand home on Lake Lucerne, seen in 1904, was built in the early 1890s for Peleg Peckham for the kingly sum of $37,500, as a wedding present for his daughter. It was long one of Orlando's showplaces as the home of citrus baron Dr. P. Phillips, who in the late 1920s owned more acreage planted in citrus than anyone else in Florida. It is listed on the National Register of Historic Places.

A view looking south on Orange Avenue about 1904 shows the San Juan Hotel on the right. About 1885, Henry Kedney of Minnesota built the first incarnation of the hotel, named the San Juan de Ulloa. In 1893, Harry L. Beeman, son of the family of chewing-gum fame, bought the hotel and extended it upwards to five stories. It lasted on the same location, in different incarnations, until the last version was destroyed by fire in 1984.

A wagon rambles through a residential section of Orange Avenue about 1906, north of Orlando's business district. In 1907, the city paid the Georgia Engineering Company to pave sections of Orange Avenue, Pine Street, Church Street, and Central Boulevard with vitrified brick, but the paving on Orange did not extend into the residential area.

A group of gentleman turkey hunters assemble for a portrait in October 1907. According to the National Wild Turkey Federation, the Florida wild turkey *(Meleagris gallopavo osceola)*, also referred to as the Osceola, is found only on the peninsula of Florida. W. E. D. Scott first described the subspecies in 1890 and named it after the famous Seminole leader.

A serious fire in 1884 had one good result: the organization of the Orlando fire department in 1885, here seen near the Oak (Wall) Street station in the department's early years. The first chief, John Weeks, had come to Orlando to work with his father-in-law, John Sinclair. Chief Weeks resigned in 1888 to return to New England, where he would become a Massachusetts senator and secretary of war in the Coolidge and Harding administrations.

"Isn't this pretty," a postcard writer scribbled about a scene on Orlando's tree-lined West Street about 1908, the year city boosters sponsored a contest to come up with a new nickname for Orlando to replace the "Phenomenal City." Suggestions included the "Magic City," the "Picturesque City," and the "Health City," but Mrs. W. S. Branch, Sr., topped them all with her suggestion, the "City Beautiful."

THE CITY BEAUTIFUL BLOOMS

(1909–1939)

By now clearly Orlando's main drag, Orange Avenue remains unpaved about 1910 in this view facing north. The buildings with the turret (left) and dome (right) are at Orange and Pine Street. The domed building was originally the home of the State Bank of Orlando, granted a charter in 1893.

Orlando Regional Medical Center's roots go back to St. Luke's Church and Home Hospital on Anderson Street (seen about 1910). When St. Luke's announced it would have to close in 1916 because of inadequate funding, Orlando doctors began a drive to build the hospital that would become Orlando General, on Kuhl Avenue (now South Orange), the genesis of Orlando Regional.

A varied group of folks enjoy fishing at Lake Lucerne about 1910, about the same time Orlando businessman Charles Lord took a trip back to his native England and had two pairs of swans, a black pair and a white pair, shipped to Orlando, where they were placed on Lake Lucerne. The city reimbursed Lord 95 dollars for the transportation costs.

In 1910, Orlandoans celebrated their first fair since the great freeze of 1894-95 with a parade down Orange Avenue featuring cars festooned with flowers. The Kanner family's flower-bedecked horse and buggy may have been decorated as a float for that parade or a similar one around 1910 or 1911.

A fine automobile sits ready to cross the St. Johns River on February 14, 1912. In the early days of auto travel, a ferry across the St. Johns provided a key route from Orlando to DeLand and other towns to the east in Volusia County. Located 27 miles from Orlando near Sanford, the ferry also offered auto-driving Orlandoans access to Daytona Beach and other Atlantic Ocean beaches, where cool breezes relieved the summer heat.

Although Orlando wouldn't become the world's theme park capital for decades, the city's weather, scenery, and access by railroads and steamboats drew winter tourists almost from the city's earliest days. These gents, members of the Tourist Quoit Club, had their photo taken downtown February 16, 1912. Pronounced "kwAits," quoits is a lawn game much like horseshoes, played with a steel disc.

Swans glide across Orlando's Lake Eola about 1915, in the early days of a tradition that continues today. First introduced at Lake Lucerne, swans soon became a fixture at Park Lake and at Lake Eola, now the city's central park. Early Orlando's most notable swan, Billy, was famed for chasing schoolchildren and was such a character generally that he remains, a fine example of taxidermy, in the collections of the Orange County Regional History Center.

Photographed January 31, 1912, a boat named the "Florence" is decorated with flowers and a flag for one of the popular floral parades that kicked off fair season in Orlando in the early years of automobile travel. The Central Florida Fair, the heir of these early expositions, now takes place later in the spring, but long reigned over Orlando in February.

Children play on the shores of Orlando's Lake Eola about 1915, just as they do today at the city's popular playground at Lake Eola Park. The site of cattle grazing in the area's earliest days of settlement in the 1850s, Orlando's focal downtown body of water was simply called "the lake" in pioneer times; the southern and eastern shores were called Sandy Beach.

Named for Orlando mayor and parks patron E. F. Sperry, the Sperry Fountain at Orlando's Lake Eola looks much the same in the twenty-first century as it did when this photograph was made about a year after its 1914 debut. The walkways were graded by Werner Nehrling, presumably the grandson of botanical pioneer Henry Nehrling, who had a large and important experimental garden near Orlando at Gotha.

Automobiles are much in evidence on a busy Orange Avenue in 1915, in this view facing south at Pine Street. The Orlando Bank and Trust Company is the turreted building on the right; the domed building on the left housed the State Bank of Orlando and Trust Company.

Photographer Seymore S. Squires captured this peaceful scene on Lake Highland about 1915. The Spanish moss hanging from trees surrounding the lake is not really moss at all, but an epiphytic member of the bromeliad family. It remains a characteristic feature of Orlando scenery.

Members of Orlando's early Jewish community were photographed at a wedding in 1916, probably at the home of the Moses Levy family, who came to the area from Pittsburgh. For the High Holy Days and other occasions, worshipers traveled on foot and by buggy and horseback to the Levy home, where services took place on the veranda. The horses were housed and fed in the Levys' orange grove.

Students at the Cathedral School for Girls near Lake Eola are dressed in white and ready for a traditional maypole ceremony on May 1, 1920. A young Tybel Burman (1908–1991) is the second girl from the left among those holding ribbons. In her later years she inspired the Tybel Burman Spivak scholarship at the University of Florida for mature women who return to college to pursue undergraduate or graduate studies.

The Kiddies' Band from Fort Meade, the first coed band in Florida, won a state band contest at Orlando, probably in the early 1920s. Fort Meade, the oldest city in Polk County, is about 75 miles from Orlando.

Employees of Orlando's first A&P grocery store stand ready to greet customers in 1925 at 235 S. Orange Avenue. Founded in 1859 as the Great American Tea Company, A&P was renamed the Great Atlantic & Pacific Tea Company in 1870, in honor of the first transcontinental railroad. By the 1920s, A&P boasted its own brands such as Sunnyfield, for bacon, butter, flour, and cereals, and Sultana, for canned goods, peanut butter, and jams.

Leonard Fox shows off merchandise including slacks, shoes, neckties, and suspenders at Leonard's Men's Shop about 1925, when the Florida land boom was at its height. In the fall of 1925, the *Orlando Morning Sentinel* valued the city's building permits for the year at more than $5.5 million, and they would go on to top almost $8.6 million—big money in times when a fine pair of shoes could be had for five dollars.

Seen in 1925, the signal tower at Orange Avenue and Central Boulevard (right) was a downtown Orlando fixture from 1925 to 1937, when it was taken down in September. The banner in the background reaching from the Beacham movie theater, at left, to the Angebilt Hotel advertises *The Lost World* starring Wallace Beery, the first film adaptation of Sir Arthur Conan Doyle's novel about a land where dinosaurs still exist.

In 1926, congregation leaders dedicate the first synagogue to be built in Orlando, for Congregation Ohev Shalom (spelled "Sholem" on the cornerstone). The building long stood at the northwest corner of East Church Street and Eola Drive, now the site of a condominium tower. The architect, George Miller, is at left; behind him is Nat Berman, one of the founders of the congregation.

Members of the Orlando High School baseball team, with 12-year-old George Wolly (front), their batboy and mascot, were photographed in 1931 in front of their relatively new honey-colored-brick building on East Robinson Street. Replacing Memorial High School, the Robinson Street campus opened in 1927 and now houses Howard Middle School. The letters "OHS" remain on one of the buildings at the edge of the block at Summerlin and East Jefferson Street.

A Florida Motor Lines bus delivers mail in 1932 to Eastern Air Transport at Orlando Municipal Airport. The field got its start in 1927, when the city arranged to purchase 33 acres north of Lake Underhill. The purchase agreement with Dr. P. Phillips, one of the best-known names in Central Florida, specified that the land should be used for general public purposes. The site remains in use as Orlando Executive Airport.

The children of the Congregation Ohev Shalom temple school gather on the steps of their synagogue in 1932. Early Jewish settlers had met in homes until 1915, when a group of families bought a small former church building at Terry Avenue and Church Street and had services there without a formal structure or rabbi. Organized in 1918, Congregation Ohev Shalom began building this synagogue at East Church Street and Eola Drive in 1926.

The landscaping around Lake Ivanhoe was transformed in the 1930s during a Works Progress Administration program. The project (not seen in this view) involved a fountain at the spot where North Orange Avenue reaches the lake and curves toward Winter Park. Upset at the cost, city comptroller W. C. Lanier called the fountain "that thing with the ball on top of it." A small replica of the Statue of Liberty stands on the site now.

One of Orlando's finest commercial photographers, Robert E. Dittrich took this 1934 image of Sergeant W. S. Singletary in the Orlando headquarters of the Florida National Guard, 124th Infantry, Third Battalion. In 1937, the city donated land for a National Guard Armory at the west end of Exposition Park, to retain the National Guard units for Orlando. The Armory was financed largely by the Works Progress Administration; the city put up $12,500 of its $80,000 cost.

Orlando's old municipal zoo on West Livingston Street near Exposition Park, here under construction in 1934, began as a Lions Club project when a club committee petitioned City Council for a zoo the same year. The Lions incorporated the nonprofit Orlando Zoological Society in December 1934, but the title remained in the city's hands.

Women card cotton in a comforter workshop during the 1930s as part of Federal Emergency Relief Administration programs in Orlando. The FERA, an early, short-lived New Deal program, was also responsible for a series of murals painted for the auditorium of the Orlando chamber of commerce building.

Orlando women make mattress comforters in 1935 as part of federal New Deal programs. That year, humorist Will Rogers noted in his syndicated column that Orlando had suspended civic eating clubs for 60 days. "This nation just naturally civic-lunched itself into the Depression," Rogers quipped. If businessmen would go home for lunch, they would be "surprised at how much more intelligently their own wife can talk than the speaker of the day! God Bless Orlando."

Writer Zora Neale Hurston (left) and Rochelle French listen in June 1935 as Gabriel Brown plays guitar in Eatonville, the small town a few miles from Orlando's center where Hurston grew up. She had long lived in the North, but she returned to Florida in the 1930s to work for the Florida Writer's Project. Also in 1935, Hurston took musicologist Alan Lomax, son of folksong collector John Lomax, on a recording expedition that began in Eatonville.

Former Governor David Sholtz makes an Orlando appearance at a barbecue and rodeo in March 1938, probably during his U.S. Senate campaign that year. Born in Brooklyn, New York, Sholtz earned his law degree at Stetson University in DeLand, about 40 miles from Orlando, and practiced law in Daytona Beach. A Democrat, he became governor in January 1933 and served one term. His inauguration was the first for a Florida governor to be broadcast on radio.

Supporters gather at the Orlando headquarters of Governor David Sholtz's Democratic-primary campaign for U.S. Senate in April 1938, in which Sholtz and Representative Mark Wilcox unsuccessfully challenged Senator Claude Pepper. According to *Time* magazine, the three toured "Florida's sticky villages and sun-blistered swamp towns, its resort cities and its inland flatwoods, to an accompaniment of loudspeakers, floodlights, bad cigars and baby-kissing such as to challenge the memory of the state's oldest inhabitant."

Leonard's Men's Shops at Orange Avenue and Church Street keeps up with the fashions of the time about 1940. A few years later Mayor Billy Beardall made an indirect comment on some men's fashions of the 1940s when he announced that all "zoot-suited" loafers would not be tolerated in the city.

From High-Flying Military Center to Haven in the Sun

(1940–1959)

Servicemen in uniform are among the guests and members of Temple Ohev Shalom, Orlando's oldest Jewish congregation, at a Passover Seder at the temple in 1943.

Soldiers march north on a brick-paved Orange Avenue during a July 4 parade in 1943 during World War II. The building behind them made its debut as the home of Dickson & Ives department store in March 1914, the same month its across-the-street rival, the Yowell-Duckworth emporium, also opened a new brick store.

About 400 servicemen and women attend a Passover Seder in 1944 at Orlando Army Air Base. That base and Pinecastle Army Airfield south of town, a training base for B-17 bomber crews, brought thousands of men and women to Orlando during World War II. Many decided to return and live in Orlando after the war. The bases also helped make the city a center of aviation in Florida and the South.

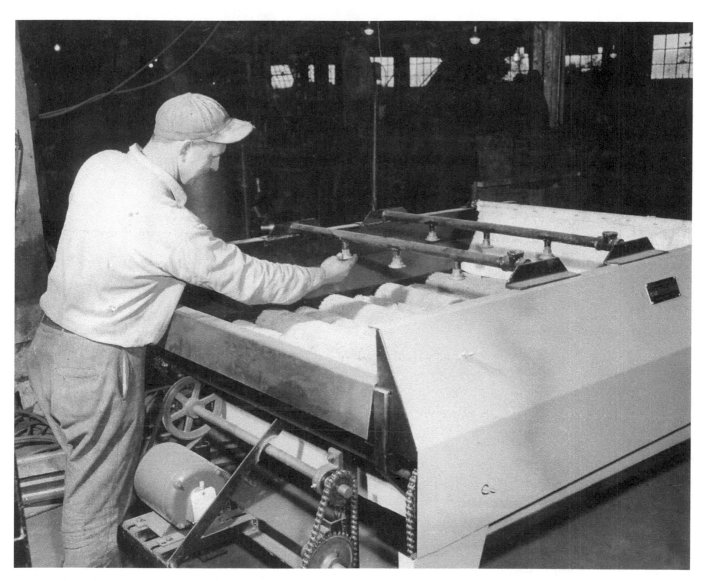

A worker adjusts a citrus polisher in 1946 in the plant of the American Machinery Corporation in Orlando. According to historian Eve Bacon, the company's Chicago Avenue plant "turned out canning, packing, fruit and vegetable-handling machinery" worth $600,000 to $700,000 during World War II. Its Fairvilla plant produced bomb casings. Bacon valued its total contribution to the war effort at $11,500,000, the highest in Orlando.

Charles Witherington and Tommy Hancock pose with a jeep about 1946. After World War II, Orlando retained a military presence at Orlando Air Force Base (later a naval training center and now Baldwin Park) and at the facility that in the 1950s became Pinecastle Air Force Base. In 1958, Pinecastle was renamed McCoy Air Force Base, after Colonel Michael McCoy, killed in 1957 in an aircraft crash with three other American and British officers.

Two men prepare for a bass-fishing expedition near Orlando about 1947, during a time when Lake Apopka to the west of Orlando reigned as a world destination for the sport. One of Florida's largest lakes, Lake Apopka is now the site of massive efforts to reverse the effects of pollution that began in the 1940s. Other Central Florida lakes remain popular bass-fishing destinations.

Men watch a demonstration of electronic logging equipment in July 1949 in an image from the Florida Geological Survey Collection.

President Harry Truman (from left), Rollins College president Hamilton Holt, and Florida governor Fuller Warren ride in an open convertible shortly after Truman's arrival in Orlando on March 8, 1949, for the dedication of the Andrews Causeway over Lake Estelle, named in honor of former U.S. senator Charles O. Andrews.

Hamilton Holt, president of Rollins College in Winter Park (left), and Florida governor Fuller Warren greet President Harry S Truman (center) on Truman's arrival in Orlando on March 8, 1949, to dedicate the Andrews Causeway across Lake Estelle between Orlando and Winter Park. A journalist and statesman before becoming Rollins' president in 1925, Holt maintained ties to many influential men and women in the arts and politics throughout his long tenure.

Members of Hadassah, a Jewish women's educational and service organization, meet in Orlando in May 1949, perhaps at a state or national convention.

Hats remained an important accessory for a well-dressed lady (and gentleman) in Orlando in the 1940s, and the Hat Box shop at 100 North Orange Avenue had the stock to prove it in 1949. In the 1940s, ladies would don hats and gloves to lunch at the Angebilt Hotel and other fashionable spots downtown.

Three judges look over entries during the National Orange Picking Contest in Orlando in 1950, when Orange County's place in the state's citrus industry was at its height. In the 1950s, more than 80,000 acres were planted in Citrus in Orange County, growers estimated, putting the county second only to Polk in the amount of citrus produced.

Young women serve juice at the National Orange Picking Contest in 1950 in front of a container that reads "Drink Yourself to Health." Orlando citrus baron Dr. P. Phillips, who died in 1959, pioneered advertising linking citrus to good health. In the 1930s, his juice labels advised customers to "Drink Dr. Phillips orange juice because the Doc says it's good for you" and touted the approval of the American Medical Association's Council on Foods.

Young women pose with the scoreboard at the National Orange Picking Contest in 1951, when citrus reigned in Orlando and Orange County. The 1950s were far from trouble-free for area growers, however; diseases and weather caused problems. In 1950 Dr. J. F. L. Childs, plant pathologist with the USDA Horticultural Laboratory in Orlando, announced his discovery that a citrus disease, Xyloporosis, was caused by a virus and was attacking tangelos in Orange County.

Reggie Moffat of the Orlando Jaycees (third from left) hands the first-place trophy to Frank Davis at the National Orange Picking Contest in February 1951, while Bill Carter (left) and Strawberry Roan look on. Carter captured third place, and Roan, second.

Shuffleboard enthusiasts compete at public courts near downtown Orlando at Sunshine Park in 1956. Sunshine Park was part of what used to be called Exposition Park, on West Livingston Street. The park had been the scene for evening recreation for residents and tourists as well as daylight activities since 1929, when the city placed lights there.

Passengers wait under an arched colonnade as a train arrives in 1957 at Orlando's passenger depot on Sligh Boulevard. Built in 1926 at a cost of nearly $500,000, the Spanish Mission station debuted in January 1927 with elaborate ceremonies. A crowd of about 6,000, about a fifth of the town's population then, jammed traffic for blocks around the building.

A band performance attracts a winter crowd at Orlando's Lake Eola Park in 1958, about a year after the city's trademark fountain in the center of the lake was dedicated. The Orlando-UCF Shakespeare Festival and many other groups continue to offer outdoor performances at the lake—now at the Walt Disney Amphitheater, which sits near the site of the bandstand in this photo.

Crowds gather in Orlando about 1957 at the groundbreaking for a hospital to serve black residents. Designed by West Palm Beach architect William Manly King, it debuted in August 1958 and had about 50 beds. The hospital was part of the Florida Sanitarium system and was funded largely by the philanthropy of Dr. P. Phillips, according to Eve Bacon's *Orlando: A Centennial History.*

Technicians test high-frequency devices in 1958 at the U.S. Naval Research Laboratory's Underwater Sound Reference facility on South Fern Creek Avenue in Orlando. The $2 million operation had been formally dedicated in June 1951, expanding on a research installation at the site during World War II, under the direction of Columbia University.

An overhead view in 1958 shows the U.S. Naval Research Laboratory's Underwater Sound Reference facility at Lake Gem Mary. The site is north of Gatlin Road between Summerlin Avenue and Lake Gem Circle and is next to the site of Fort Gatlin, the Seminole War fort that inspired the beginnings of Orlando. Established in 1838, Fort Gatlin overlooked three lakes, in an area that pioneers said was frequented by Seminole leaders.

A large sonar dome is lowered into Lake Gem Mary at the U.S. Naval Research Laboratory's Underwater Sound Reference facility in 1958. The facility closed in the late 1990s. Also called Deep Lake, Lake Gem Mary was chosen for research because of its depth (about 35 feet) and clear water.

The Martin Company missile plant south of Orlando, here in 1958, marked an important milestone in the city's history. Martin officials signed a contract to purchase 6,777 acres for $1.95 million in 1956, and the plant opened in December 1957. Later Martin Marietta, it is now part of Lockheed Martin. In the 1950s, Martin was building the Vanguard booster rocket, and the company needed a manufacturing facility close to Cape Canaveral.

Connected by covered walkways, the concrete-block buildings of Audubon Park Elementary, here in 1956, resemble many schools built in Central Florida during the postwar growth years of the 1950s. The school's address is on Falcon Drive; not surprisingly, the names of the streets in the Audubon Park subdivision were named for birds.

Governor Leroy Collins (left) talks with James H. Douglas, secretary of the U.S. Air Force, in 1958 at a Military Appreciation Dinner in Orlando. Florida's governor from January 4, 1955, to January 3, 1961, Collins was honored by the legislature as the "Floridian of the Century" on his death in 1991.

An employee of Southern Bell Telephone and Telegraph Company in Orlando shows off the latest computerized equipment in July 1959 in what was touted as the company's first completely mechanized accounting office.

Orlando's trademark fountain provides a backdrop for folks strolling in Lake Eola Park in 1958. The fountain debuted October 5, 1957, the day after Soviet scientists launched *Sputnik* into space. "Russia may have its earth satellite, but Orlando for the last two days seems to have been more interested in its new Centennial fountain," news reports declared October 6. The fountain's dedication marked the 100th anniversary of Orlando as the county seat.

America's Vacation Land

(1960–1974)

This rooftop view of the changing Orlando skyline about 1960 shows the courthouse annex at right that replaced Orange County's 1892 red-brick Victorian courthouse. The small Corner Canteen (center) stood at Central Boulevard and Magnolia Avenue, now the site of the southwest corner of the Orlando public library.

Seen in 1960, Tupperware Home Parties' national headquarters was built in the mid-1950s on the company's land just north of Kissimmee, but it continued to have an Orlando address. Under the direction of sales chief Brownie Wise (who resigned in 1958), Tupperware quickly became the country's premier direct seller. "If we build the people," Wise famously said, "they'll build the business."

Tupperware Home Parties' sales representatives, dressed as "spacettes," pose before the entranceway to its headquarters during the company's 1960 sales jubilee. In the 1950s and 1960s, the Tupperware home party emerged as a woman's domain in a business world in which many doors were closed to women. The driving force behind Tupperware Home Parties, Brownie Wise, was the first woman to appear on the cover of *Business Week*.

A colonnade of pastel missiles lines the entranceway to the headquarters of Tupperware Home Parties near Orlando in 1960. The Space Age was the theme for the company's annual sales jubilee, a celebration for more than 1,200 top sales personnel. Orlando's proximity to what is now the Kennedy Space Center at Cape Canaveral put space exploration at the forefront of public awareness in Central Florida.

Onlookers watch other Tupperware sales representatives fill in the outline of a huge canvas with paint, during one of the Fun Day events during the 1960 sales jubilee at the headquarters of Tupperware Home Parties near Orlando. The grounds of the Kissimmee campus still contain reminders of early jubilees. The Garden That Loyalty Built honored 4,000 Tupperware dealers who met recruiting goals in 1954.

The monument of a Confederate soldier stands watch over the east side of Lake Eola Park in 1964, when the phone towers on top of the Southern Bell building across the lake marked the tallest point in the city's skyline. Originally placed at a downtown intersection in 1911 by the United Daughters of the Confederacy, the statue was moved to its park location in 1917.

Democratic gubernatorial candidate Farris Bryant (at the microphone) gets a hand from other statewide party nominees during a campaign stop in Orlando in 1960 in the days when winning the Democratic nomination for a statewide office in Florida was almost tantamount to being elected—although Republican Richard Nixon did top John F. Kennedy in the state's presidential vote in 1960.

The entrance to Gatorland, one of the Orlando area's oldest attractions, welcomes visitors in the early 1960s. Gatorland has roots in the 1950s, but the gaping gator entrance dates from 1962, when founder Owen Godwin's youngest son, Frank, designed it in his father's favorite color scheme: Florida aqua and white. A beloved landmark for longtime area residents, the jaws and the attraction survived a serious fire in late 2006.

Workers load boats built by the Orlando Boat Company in 1963. The Orlando area's many lakes made it a natural spot for enthusiasts of boating and water sports. With the fourth and fifth generations of the Meloon family active in the business, Orlando-based Correct Craft, which began in 1925, claims the distinction of being the oldest family-owned boat company in the nation.

Roy Disney (on pier, second from left, with glasses), brother of Walt Disney, and other Disney officials visit property that would soon become Walt Disney World, probably in February 1967. The acquisition of parcels to make up the site of Walt Disney World in the mid-1960s marked one of the greatest secret land deals in Florida history.

Roy Disney (left, with glasses) and other Disney officials tour their Florida property by boat, probably during a February 1967 site inspection. Much of the property consisted of wetland, and the company built more than 40 miles of canals, 18 miles of levees, and 13 water-control structures, according to Richard E. Foglesong's *Married to the Mouse: Walt Disney World and Orlando*.

The 1960 Orange County courthouse annex, photographed in 1964, stood on the site that is now Heritage Square, by the Orange County Regional History Center. Though the annex came from the drawing boards of respected architects, many Orlandoans thought it looked like something that belonged on a beachfront rather than downtown. It was razed in the late 1990s.

On one of the most significant days in Orlando's history, Walt Disney (from left), retired General William "Joe" Potter, and Roy Disney smile for many cameras at the November 15, 1965, press conference at the Egyptian Room of the Cherry Plaza hotel at which Walt Disney announced plans to build something bigger and better than California's Disneyland, near Orlando. This was Walt Disney's only public appearance in Orlando. He died 13 months later.

Cabinet members, state legislators, and a delegation of Disney representatives from California joined Roy Disney and Florida governor Claude Kirk in Orlando on May 12, 1967, for the ceremonial signing of complex legislation granting the Walt Disney Company governmental powers and immunities and creating the Reedy Creek Improvement District, the company's governmental arm.

In the 1960s, few Central Floridians could have imagined that one of the world's most famous entertainment pioneers would inspire the purchase of a piece of raw Florida land larger than Manhattan and transform it into an international icon: Walt Disney World in Orlando. Here Disney officials inspect their Orlando land, probably during a site visit in early 1967, after Walt Disney's death in December 1966.

An aerial view shows the site of Walt Disney World in June 1967, soon after the Florida legislature accommodated the Disney organization by creating the Reedy Creek Improvement District. William "Joe" Potter, a retired Army Corps of Engineers general, headed the district, which was responsible for building Walt Disney World's utilities and public works.

Under bright (and hot) summer skies, a group of officers show off a Florida Highway Patrol "Eye in the Sky" plane at Orlando in August 1967.

Flanked by Secret Service guards, Richard M. Nixon makes a campaign stop in Orlando on September 18, 1968, during his tumultuous race against Democratic Vice-president Hubert Humphrey and American Independent candidate George Wallace of Alabama, who drew 46 electoral votes (to Nixon's 301 and Humphrey's 191). Several years later, in November 1973, Nixon would make his famous "I am not a crook" speech in Orlando, at a gathering of Associated Press managing editors.

Walt Disney World's Magic Kingdom is seen from the air in September 1971, soon before it opened October 1. To construct the park, the Disney workforce created a mile-wide lake, Seven Seas Lagoon, which was lined with millions of gallons of white sand.

A group of "trip hostesses" for the Walt Disney Company were photographed January 28, 1970, before the opening of the Magic Kingdom on October 1, 1971. The Disney company's initial Florida offices were in the venerable Metcalf Building in downtown Orlando.

The Contemporary Hotel at Walt Disney's Magic Kingdom, with its entrance for the monorail that connected parts of the theme park, looks like something from the park's Tomorrowland on its opening in 1971.

Early visitors gaze at Cinderella's Castle, the centerpiece of the Magic Kingdom at Walt Disney World, probably on opening day: October 1, 1971. Walt Disney's parents were married in Florida on January 1, 1888, near what today is Paisley, about 45 miles from Orlando. The couple soon moved to Daytona Beach, where their oldest son, Herbert, was born. They later moved to Chicago, where Walt was born in 1901.

Visitors flock into the Magic Kingdom, the first part of Walt Disney World to open, in October 1971. Epcot, MGM Studios, Animal Kingdom, water parks, hotels, nightclubs, and restaurants were added in later years. By the mid-1990s, more than a billion people had passed through the gates of Disney's Florida creation.

Ski lifts carry visitors over a street in Fantasyland at Disney's Magic Kingdom soon after the park's opening in October 1971. Cinderella's Golden Carousel is at left. Like Disneyland in California, the Magic Kingdom contains several "lands": Tomorrowland, Adventureland, Frontierland, and Fantasyland, all well known nationwide when the park opened because of the popular Disney television programs that began in 1954 and were introduced by Walt Disney himself until his death in December 1966.

An authentic steam-powered sternwheeler sits near Liberty Square across from the Hall of Presidents (at right) near the Haunted Mansion in the Frontierland section of Disney's Magic Kingdom early in the 1970s. The original steamboat was named the *Admiral Joe Fowler*, after the real-life retired admiral who guided construction at both Disneyland in California and Walt Disney World.

An evening view in 1973 shows an illuminated Lake Eola Park's Centennial Fountain, which changes colors at night. Landscape architect William C. Pauley of Atlanta designed and engineered the plastic and concrete dome, which sits on pilings using 28 steel cylinders that were driven into the lake bottom.

An animal trainer rides two dolphins during the "Isle of Dolphins" show at SeaWorld in Orlando. The adult admission charge was $4.50 when the park opened in December 1973; tickets for children between the ages of four and twelve cost $2. The first family to visit the attraction was offered a lifetime pass for free admission.

An aerial view of SeaWorld in Orlando in its early days. When the attraction opened in December 1973, it featured a show called "Fountain Fantasy," which mixed spouting water, lights, music, and slides in a 900-foot auditorium.

Two sea lions perform an aquatic barrel-roll under a trainer's direction at SeaWorld in Orlando, perhaps on the theme park's opening day: December 15, 1973. This may be an act in what was called the "Ding-A-Ling Brothers Seal and Penguin Circus" in ads for SeaWorld's opening.

"Shamu" bestows a kiss on a young woman at SeaWorld's Orlando attraction during the park's early days in the 1970s. The first orca, or killer whale, brought to SeaWorld's original San Diego, California, park in the 1960s was named Shamu, and the moniker has remained the stage name for the theme park's stars, several killer whales that have their own individual names off-stage.

A dolphin performs a jump at SeaWorld's theme park in Orlando. On the park's opening day in 1973, news reports said its water shows took place in two stadia, each of which seated 34,000.

The "Florida Hurricane," a roller coaster at the now-gone Circus World attraction west of Orlando, thrills riders in the late 1970s. Opening in 1974 as Circus World Showcase, the park added the coaster later, when it was owned by the giant toymaker Mattel. In the 1980s, the attraction became part of the Boardwalk and Baseball theme park, owned then by Orlando-based textbook publishers Harcourt, Brace and Jovanovich.

A sign welcomes visitors to the Hawaiian Punch Village on opening day at SeaWorld in Orlando. The well-landscaped new attraction also had a Japanese village area, the *Orlando Sentinel-Star* reported.

A view of Orlando's Orange Avenue looking north about 1974 shows several lost landmarks, including the American Fire & Casualty building at right and the Downtowner Motor Inn at left, in front of the SunBank building that has been replaced by the 32-story SunTrust Tower. In this view, the 18-story CNA building, which opened in 1971 and houses the venerable Citrus Club, stands as the city's tallest.

Notes on the Photographs

These notes, listed by page number, attempt to include all aspects known of the photographs. Each of the photographs is identified by the page number, a title or description, photographer and collection, archive, and call or box number when applicable. Although every attempt was made to collect all data, in some cases complete data may have been unavailable due to the age and condition of some of the photographs and records.

9 781683 368687